Science Experiments

WITH

SOUND

Sally Nankivell-Aston
and Dorothy Jackson

W

FRANKLIN WATTS
LONDON • SYDNEY

This edition 2003

Franklin Watts
96 Leonard Street, London EC2A 4XD

Franklin Watts Australia
45-51 Huntley Street
Alexandria
NSW 2015

Editor: Claire Berridge
Art director: Jonathan Hair
Designer: Mo Choy
Picture research: Susan Mennell
Photography: Ray Moller, unless
otherwise acknowledged
Artwork: Peter Bull

A CIP catalogue record for this book
is available from the British Library.

ISBN 0 7496 3602 5

Dewey Classification 537

Printed in Malaysia

Acknowledgements:
Cover: Steve Shott; Tony Stone Images 4 (tr Tom Tietz;
mc Tim Davis), 25 (tl Chuck Davis), 29 (bl MacNeal
Hospital); Tony Stone Worldwide 14 (bl Mike Vines);
Rex Features 4 (mr Nils Jorgensen), 11 (bl Nils
Jorgensen) 18 (bl Alix/Panie) 23 (mr); Image Bank 5
(bl Don Klumpp), 17 (mr Steve Niedorf), 27 (bl Jamie
Villaseca); The Stock Market 8 (bl Ned Gillette), 12 (bl
Jean Miele); Science Photo Library 21 (mr Charles D.
Winters).

Thanks, too, to our models: Nicola Blackman, Mica
Dhyll, Aaron Gupta, George Marney, Thomas Sipi,
Ahmani Vidal-Simon, Beau-Bart Von Haidenthaler,
David Watts and Amy Willoughby.

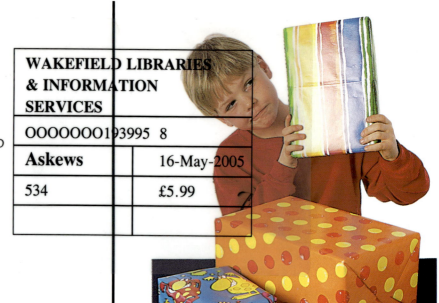

Contents

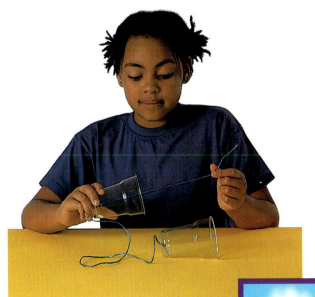

Sounds all around

IT IS VERY DIFFICULT TO IMAGINE a world without sound. Our world is full of lots of different sounds, some you will like, some you won't, some that are natural, some that are made by people or machines. Some sounds are made for a reason – to communicate, to give pleasure or to warn of danger. Other sounds just happen. All sounds are caused by something vibrating. We hear the sounds because the vibrations travel through the air to our ears.

What is the source of sound in each picture? Can you describe the different sounds you would hear from each sound source?

Be amazed

By doing the experiments in this book you can learn some amazing things about sound. You will find out how sounds behave, how we hear them and lots of other interesting facts. Some experiments may answer questions that you already ask about sound. Some may make you think of more!

Look closely

Scientists always ask lots of questions and observe carefully. That includes looking, feeling and listening. When you are doing the experiments, look closely to see what is happening. Don't be upset if your predictions do not always turn out to be correct as scientists (and that includes you!) learn a lot from unexpected results.

Be careful

Always make sure an adult knows that you are doing an experiment. Ask for help if you need to cut, saw or to use heavy, sharp or electrical items. Very loud sounds can damage your hearing, so be careful. Follow the step-by-step instructions carefully and remember – be a safe scientist!

Sound detectives

When you are given presents on your birthday, have you ever tried to guess what is inside before you unwrap them? If the present is in a box, then it is difficult to get clues by looking at the shape. So, you might listen to the sounds made by the object inside as you move the present around. Find out how good a friend is at guessing what is inside some mystery boxes.

❶ Make 4 mystery boxes by putting one object inside each box, and then wrap the boxes with the paper.

In action

Special sound effects are made for plays in schools and theatres and on the radio. Often the object used to make the sound effect is nothing like the real sound source!

❷ Give the boxes to your friend and ask him or her to listen to the sounds made by the object inside as he or she tips each box gently from side to side. Do the sounds tell them about the way the objects move? Which objects roll? Which objects slide? Can any slide and roll?

3 Ask your friend to turn the box over and over. What sound does each object make when it drops inside the box? Which objects sound heavy and which sound light?

Keep thinking

When you cross a road you are told to stop, look and listen. What sorts of sounds would tell you it was unsafe to cross? What noise do you hear when large vehicles are reversing? Why do you think they make this noise?

4 Now ask your friend to shake the boxes. What sound does each object make when shaken? Using these sound clues, can they guess what object is inside each box?

5 Open the mystery boxes and find out! Is your friend good at being a sound detective?

Don't stop there

● Use a tape recorder to make a cassette tape of different everyday sounds that you can hear around your home or school. Play the tape to some friends and find out how many of the sounds they can identify.

● Sit in a garden or school playground. Close your eyes for 10 minutes and listen carefully. Make a list of all the sounds you hear. Which sounds do you like? Which do you dislike?

Seeing sound

SOUND IS NOT SOMETHING that you can see - you only hear it. However, by doing the following experiment, you can 'see' the effect of sound vibrations. Make sure you get permission from an adult to do this experiment.

✔ **you will need**
- ✔ a stereo system with loudspeakers
- ✔ a metal tin (without lid)
- ✔ rice
- ✔ a tape or CD of dance music

1 Put one of the loudspeakers on its back. Place the tin upside-down on top of the speaker, over the place where the sound comes out.

2 Now put some rice on top of the upside-down tin.

 In action

Sometimes sound vibrations can be very useful. In many ski resorts the vibrations from the sound of an explosion are used to start avalanches deliberately during the night so that slopes are safe for skiers the next morning.

3 Play some dance music on your stereo system. Choose a track that has a heavy beat (bass line) in it. Play the music quietly at first then slowly turn up the volume until the rice dances to the music!

4 What happens if you turn the volume up a bit more? What do the rice grains do now? Be careful – if the music is too loud it could damage your hearing. Why do you think the rice dances in this way?

Don't stop there

● Find out what other things 'dance' to the music. Repeat the experiment using foods such as sugar, salt, cornmeal, flour or small sugar cake decorations. Which type of food 'dances' best?

● You can also see the effect of sound vibrations using a tuning fork. Hold the fork at one end and bang the forked end on a table edge. Quickly put the forked end into a bowl of water. What do you notice?

Feeling sound

Y OU CAN FEEL SOUND vibrations as well as seeing the effect of them. Some people who are deaf dance in time to music by feeling the vibrations sounds make. Find out more about the feel of sound in this experiment.

✔ you will need
✔ a large round balloon

1 Blow up the balloon and tie it. Hold it by the knot.

2 Ask a friend to put his or her hand against one side of the balloon.

3 Put your mouth against the other side of the balloon. Say the letters of the alphabet slowly and clearly.

4 Find out which of the sounds your friend can feel most easily. You might like to record your results in a table. What is the sound travelling through inside the balloon?

Don't stop there

● Now fill a balloon with water and do the experiment again. Can you still feel the vibrations from the sounds? Can sound travel through water?

● Cut open a large balloon (that has not been blown up) and stretch it over one end of a long cardboard tube. Hold it in place with sticky tape. Put your hand on the balloon and talk into the other end of the tube. Can you feel the vibrations?

In action

Evelyn Glennie is a world-famous percussionist. She is also deaf but manages to 'hear' music by feeling the vibrations made by the instruments.

Keep thinking

There is a special alarm clock for people who are deaf. Instead of ringing, the clock vibrates. Where do you think people who use this type of clock put it during the night, so the vibrations wake them up in the morning?

Sound on the move

SOUND VIBRATIONS TRAVEL through the air in waves. The experiment below will give you a good idea of how these waves of sound travel. The Slinky represents a sound wave.

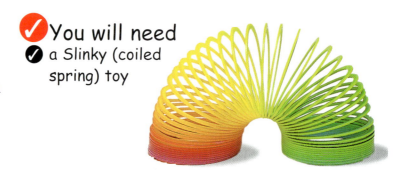

1 Ask a friend to hold one end of the Slinky and stretch it across the top of a table. Hold the other end yourself.

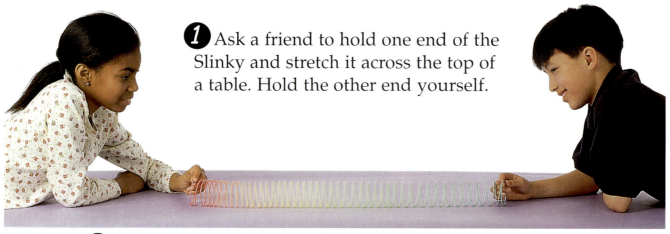

2 Quickly pull your end of the Slinky backwards and forwards, in a sharp movement. In this way you are acting like a vibrating sound source. Look closely to see what happens. Can you see a wave travelling from your end of the Slinky to the other end?

In action

Vibrations from sound waves that travel through the ground in earthquakes are recorded on special machines called seismographs. Scientists monitor movement of the Earth's surface on these machines so that they can have some idea of when earthquakes are going to occur.

3 Send another wave along the Slinky in the same way as before. Make sure you don't lift the Slinky off the table. Look closely to see what happens to the coils as the wave travels along.

4 Watch what happens when the wave reaches your friend's end. Does the wave travel in one direction and then come back? Can you make it come all the way back?

Don't stop there

● When an object vibrates more quickly, the sound waves travelling from it are more frequent. Watch what happens to the Slinky when you send several waves, one straight after another.

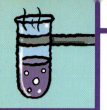

Speed of sound

WHEN YOU HEAR THE BELL ring or the whistle blow at the end of playtime at school, you seem to hear the sound straight away. This is because sound travels quickly from the source of the sound to your ears. Find out more about the speed of sound and how quickly it travels over different distances in this experiment.

1 Do this experiment in a quiet open space. Ask two friends to stand in the middle of your chosen space. Give the drum to one friend (the drummer). Give the scarf to the other (the listener). Ask the listener to walk 20 paces away from the drummer.

2 Stand back so you can see both friends clearly.

In action

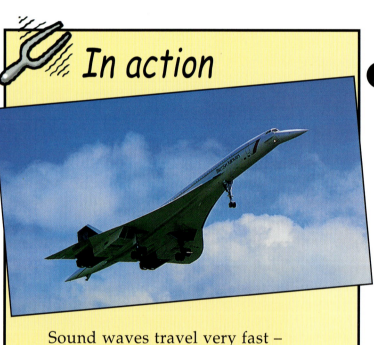

Sound waves travel very fast – about 340 metres per second in air. But Concorde can travel even faster! At take-off Concorde builds up speed, getting faster and faster until it breaks the sound barrier. It is then travelling even faster than the speed of sound! We call this supersonic speed.

3 Do you think there is a noticeable time gap between a sound being made and a sound being heard? Find out by asking the drummer to bang the drum and the listener to raise the scarf as soon as she/he hears the drum (without looking!). Listen and look closely to see if the drum beat is heard at the same time it is made. Repeat this step 3 times. What happens?

4 Now ask the listener to walk 20 more paces away from the drummer and repeat the experiment. Does the listener seem to hear the sound as soon as it is made, even when the sound is further away? What does this tell you about the speed of sound?

Don't stop there

● Now put a ringing alarm clock in the middle of the open space and slowly walk away from it. What happens to the sound? Does it get louder, softer or stay the same as you get further away? Walk in a circle around the clock, keeping the same distance away from it this time. Does the sound spread out from the clock in all directions?

How do we hear sounds?

WE HEAR SOUNDS WITH OUR EARS. Our outer ear 'collects' the sound waves and funnels them down the ear canal. The sound reaches the eardrum, making it vibrate. This, in turn, causes three tiny ear bones in our middle ear to vibrate. Then little hairs in part of the inner ear called the cochlea vibrate. A special nerve then sends these 'vibration' messages to the brain (see diagram on page 17 opposite). Try this experiment to find out more about hearing.

✓ **you will need**
✓ a tuning fork

1 Ask a friend to sit on a chair in a very quiet place, away from any distracting sounds.

2 Take the tuning fork and bang the forked end on a table edge. The tuning fork will vibrate and make a musical note.

3 Quickly put the end you are holding against your friend's head, near the entrance to the ear canal. Can your friend hear the note made by the tuning fork? Can he or she hear it well?

4 Repeat this two or three times. How is the sound being heard?

5 Now twang the tuning fork again in the same way as before. This time quickly put the end of the fork on your friend's head, about 5 cm behind the outer ear. Predict what will happen. Can your friend hear the note now? Does it sound the same as it did before? What do you think is happening?

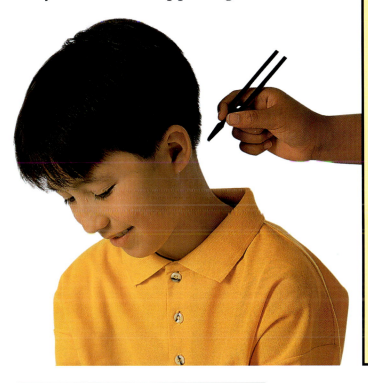

In action

There are many reasons why some people cannot hear very well. One common reason, especially in children, is 'glue ear'. Sticky fluid builds up in the middle ear. This stops the ear drum and ear bones vibrating properly so sounds cannot be heard well.

Doctors use an instrument called an auriscope (or otoscope) which has a light and a lens, to help them examine people's ears.

Don't stop there

● Ask your friend to repeat the experiment to see if you can hear the note as well in front of, as behind your ear.

● How good is your hearing? Find out by measuring how far away you can hear a pin drop.

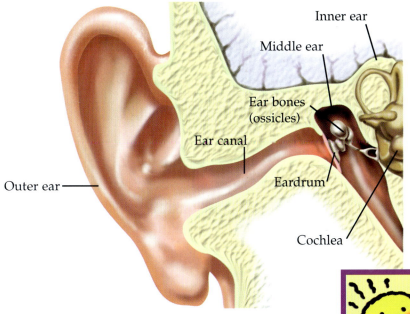

Inner ear

Middle ear

Ear bones (ossicles)

Ear canal

Outer ear

Eardrum

Cochlea

Improve your hearing!

DO YOU REMEMBER THE STORY of Little Red Riding Hood? When she saw the wolf in her grandmother's clothes she exclaimed, 'Grandmother, what big ears you have.' The wolf replied, 'All the better to hear you with!' Do you think having big ears helps you hear better? Make some big ears and experiment with them to find out.

✔ **you will need**
- ✓ a large piece of thin card
- ✓ sticky tape
- ✓ a radio

1 Use the card to make a large cone 'ear' to fit over one of your ears.

2 Turn the radio on very low. Sit a short distance away and listen carefully.

In action

Animal horns used to be used to help people hear better, and the first ear trumpets were made in a similar shape. These simple hearing aids used the cone shape to channel the sounds into the ear so people could hear more clearly. Hearing aids are now much more sophisticated. They consist of a miniature microphone, amplifier and loudspeaker.

3 Hold the 'big ear' close to one of your ears. Sit in the same place as before and listen to the radio again with your big ear turned towards it. What do you notice about the sound? Does it sound louder, softer, different in any way, or just the same?

4 Try the test a few times to be sure! Did your 'big ear' improve your hearing?

Keep thinking

Have you seen a doctor use a stethoscope? What do you think they are used for?

Don't stop there

● Do you think the size of the 'ear' will make a difference to the loudness of the sound? Try making an even bigger 'ear' and a much smaller one. Do the experiment again using each one. What did you find out?

● Do you think the shape of the ear will make a difference to the sound you hear? Try the experiment with ears of different shapes, such as a narrow, pointed one and a short, rounded one. Don't forget to do all the tests in the same way to keep it fair. Did the shape of the ear make a difference to the sound you heard?

Loud and soft

THINK ABOUT HOW YOU MAKE loud sounds or soft sounds. The mine workers in South Africa make loud and soft sounds to accompany a dance using decorated rubber boots. You and your friends can make some decorated boots too, and do your own rubber-boot dance!

✔ **you will need**
- ✓ a length of elastic (about 1 metre)
- ✓ a pair of rubber boots to fit you
- ✓ strong thread
  a selection of items that can be tied onto the boots to make sounds – such as buttons, washers, small bells, beads and paper clips

1 Cut two lengths of elastic, each one long enough to fit around the leg of the boot with enough extra so that you can tie it on.

2 Tie a piece of elastic fairly tightly around the leg of each boot.

3 Use loops of thread and paper clips to tie the bells, washers etc. in bundles along the lengths of elastic. Make sure each one can swing freely.

4 Stamp your feet gently and listen to the sound you make. Is it loud or soft? Stamp harder and listen to the sound now. Is it different?

5 Do the 'rubber-boot' dance by dancing and stamping about. Find out what you can do to make loud or soft sounds. Try to make different sounds, for example soft drizzle, rain and then a storm.

In action

An oscilloscope shows how a sound wave changes. The picture shows the amplitude (the height) of the sound wave, and how this changes as the sound changes. A tall wave shows a loud sound and a short wave shows a quieter sound. You may have noticed on some machines like CD and cassette players that there is a coloured light display. Lights 'move' up and down as the sound gets louder and softer.

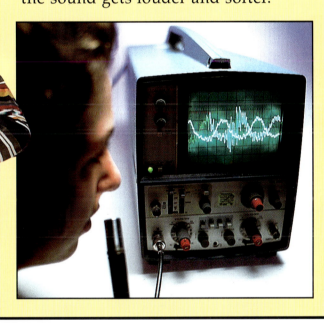

Don't stop there

● Use junk materials to help you make a very loud clap of thunder. Use the thunder sound and the wellies to create the sound effects for a story about a developing storm.

High and low

IN SOUTH AMERICA, PEOPLE PLAY a musical instrument called the pan-pipes. Lots of different notes from high to low can be played on these pipes. Find out about making high and low notes when you make and decorate your very own pan-pipes.

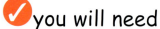
1 Ask an adult to cut the pipe with the hacksaw into a range of lengths from long to short.

2 Arrange the pieces of pipe next to each other, in order of length. Tape them together and then decorate them.

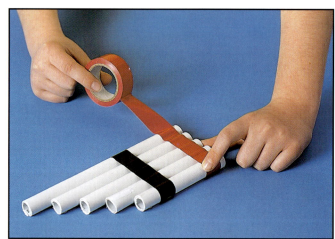

Keep thinking

Some animals, such as dogs, can hear higher pitched sounds than we can. There is a whistle that dogs hear but it has too high a pitch for us to hear. Why do you think this might be useful?

Sound waves of high pitched notes have a higher frequency than low pitched notes. Look back to pages 12-13 where you used the Slinky to see how sound waves travel. The 'quick' waves had a higher frequency.

3 First blow over the top of the long pipe. You may need to practise to get a good note.

4 Now blow over the next pipe that is a little bit shorter. What do you notice about the sound? Is the note higher or lower?

5 What kind of note do you think the next pipe will make? Try it and see if you were right. Try blowing over all the other pipes. What do you notice about the notes? Use your pan-pipes to make up your own tunes.

6 A note which sounds higher or lower than another has a different pitch or frequency. Why do you think the pitch is different for each pipe?

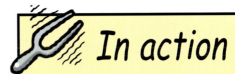

In action

Many instruments have tubes of different lengths to change the pitch of the sound. The pitch is changed in a trombone by sliding the tube to make it longer or shorter.

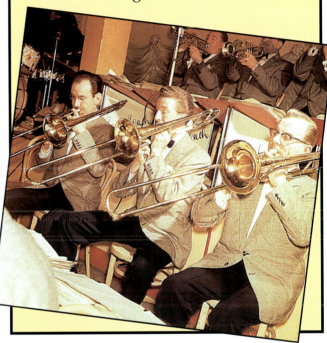

Don't stop there

● Some instruments have strings which are plucked to make notes. Find some empty cartons in different sizes, some large and some small. Remove the lids and stretch an elastic band over each carton. Twang each band and listen carefully to hear the sound it makes. What do you notice about the pitch of the notes from each band?

What does sound travel through?

SOUND TRAVELS THROUGH THE AIR (which is a gas) and this is usually how the sounds we hear come into our ears. But will sound also travel through solid things like string? In this experiment you can make a simple telephone and find out more about what sound travels through.

✔ **you will need**
- ✔ two plastic cups
- ✔ a sharp tool like a skewer or scissors
- ✔ string (about 3 metres)

❶ Ask an adult to help you make a small hole in the base of each cup with the sharp tool.

❷ Thread one end of the string through one cup and tie a knot in it, on the inside of the cup. Thread the other end through the other cup and tie it in the same way.

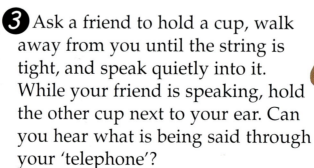
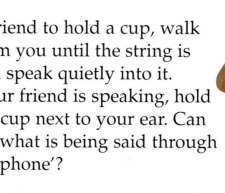

❸ Ask a friend to hold a cup, walk away from you until the string is tight, and speak quietly into it. While your friend is speaking, hold the other cup next to your ear. Can you hear what is being said through your 'telephone'?

In action

Some sea creatures like dolphins (or whales) send sounds through many miles of ocean. They can do this because sound travels so well through water, faster in fact, than it does through air.

4 Move closer to your friend and try the 'telephone' again when the string is not pulled tight. Does your telephone work as well?

5 Ask two more friends to join you and make another 'telephone'. Link the strings together to make a cross in the centre and pull the strings tight. Speak into your cup and ask your friends to hold their cups to their ears. Does the sound travel along each of the strings?

Don't stop there

● Make a simple stethoscope using a length of plastic hose (or tubing) and two funnels. Push one funnel into each end of the hose and use your stethoscope to listen to a friend's heart. Can you hear the heart beat? What did the sound travel through to get to your ear?

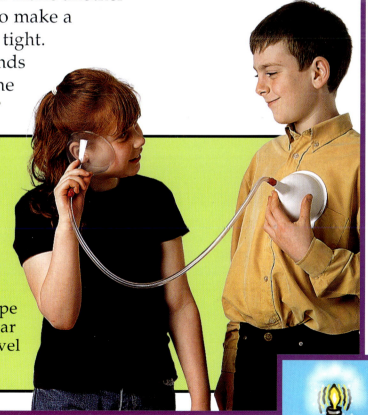

Stop that noise!

SOMETIMES IT IS NECESSARY to stop sound from travelling – for instance if the sound is so loud that it could be dangerous, or maybe because the sound is irritating. Would you like peace and quiet to do your homework? Make some ear muffs and find out which material is best to stop that noise!

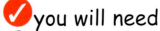
you will need
- a personal stereo with headphones
- a variety of materials such as fabrics, plastic sheeting, aluminium foil and cork mats

1 Put the headphones on and turn the stereo on so you can hear the music clearly. (SAFETY! Very loud sounds can damage your ears.)

2 Think about which of your materials will be good at stopping the sound and arrange them in order of the best to the least sound-proof.

Keep thinking

Think about who might need to protect their ears from loud noises. How do they do it?

3 Choose one material and place a piece of the same thickness next to each ear. Hold it in place with the headphones. Try the other materials in the same way.

4 Keep a record of your results – good to poor sound-proofing! Did any material stop the sound completely? Which materials stopped the most sound? Which stopped the least?

5 When sound waves reach a material, some are absorbed and some are reflected away. Only some of the sound gets through. What sort of materials let the most sound through?

Don't stop there

● Try putting a ticking clock in an empty box. Use different materials to line the box. Put on the lid and listen each time. Find out which material is best at stopping the sound.

In action

Loud sounds can be dangerous. Any sound above 140 decibels (the unit of measure for sound) will permanently damage your ears. People who work in very noisy environments, like machine workshops, have to protect their ears. Buildings are often protected from sound with double-glazed windows. The space between the panes of thick glass prevents as much sound as possible from coming through.

Bouncing sound

Y OU HAVE PROBABLY BOUNCED a ball, but did you know that you can bounce sound too, by reflecting the sound waves? This is known as an echo. Try this experiment and find out more about how sound can be bounced.

1 Start by making 2 long tubes of about 8 cm in diameter, by rolling up each piece of card and securing the loose flap with the tape.

Keep thinking

Ships at sea use fog-horns when it is foggy to find out if there is anything dangerous ahead, such as a cliff or rocks that they might crash into. How do you think an echo can help them?

2 Lean the metal tray on the table up against a wall and arrange the two long tubes on the table so that they are both at about 45 degrees to the wall.

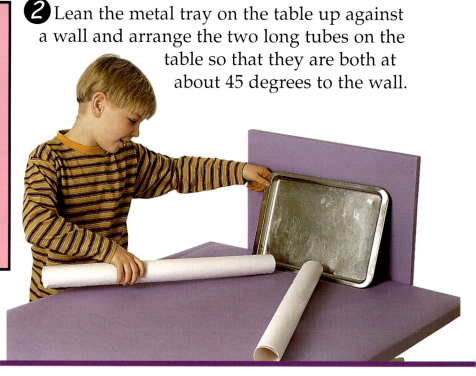

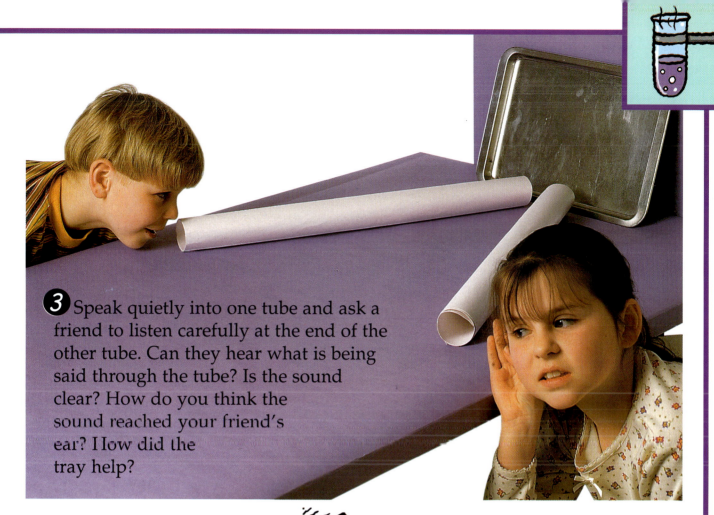

3 Speak quietly into one tube and ask a friend to listen carefully at the end of the other tube. Can they hear what is being said through the tube? Is the sound clear? How do you think the sound reached your friend's ear? How did the tray help?

Don't stop there

● When you are next in a large empty hall or tunnel shout loudly (if you are allowed to!). What do you hear? What do you think is happening to the sound of your voice?

In action

Sound waves we cannot hear, called ultrasound, are used in hospitals to show a picture of a baby inside a mother's womb. The sound waves bounce off the baby and back to a machine that shows the picture on a screen.

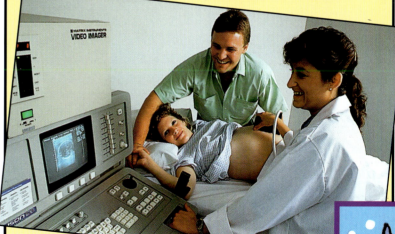

Glossary

This glossary gives the meaning of each word as it is used in this book

Absorb A material that absorbs sound soaks it up, and stops some or all of it travelling any further.

Air An invisible mixture of gases, mainly nitrogen and oxygen. Air surrounds the Earth.

Amplifier A machine to make sounds louder.

Amplitude The height of a sound wave. High amplitude sounds are loud and low amplitude sounds are soft.

Auriscope A medical device used to look inside the ear.

Avalanche A sudden or fast flow of snow or ice down a mountain.

Cochlea The part of the inner ear that converts sound vibrations into messages that are sent by nerves to the brain.

Decibel The loudness of a sound is measured on the Decibel scale.

Ear The organ that enables us to hear sounds and to keep our balance. It consists of three parts – outer, middle and inner ear.

Ear bones Three tiny bones in the middle ear that vibrate when sound waves hit the eardrum.

Ear canal Part of the outer ear. Sound waves travel down this tube to the middle ear.

Eardrum Separates the outer ear from the middle ear. It is a thin membrane (skin) which vibrates when sound waves hit it.

Ear flap The outer part of the ear on the side of your head (also called pinna or auricle). It 'collects' sound waves and channels them into the ear canal.

Earthquake Sudden sharp movements along fault lines in the Earth's crust, which often cause severe damage.

Echo A sound which is reflected and bounces back to you so you can hear it again.

Frequency The number of waves that travel past a certain point every second. The higher the frequency of a sound the higher its pitch.

Gas A gas has no fixed shape or volume. It spreads to fill a container. Often you cannot see gas.

Hearing aid A device used to improve the hearing of partially deaf people by making sounds louder.

Heartbeat The sound your heart makes when it pumps blood around your body.

Liquid A liquid has a definite volume but it can flow and take the shape of the container it is in.
Loud Sounds with high amplitude. Loud sounds have tall sound waves.
Loudspeaker A machine which converts electrical signals into sound.

Microphone A device that converts sound waves into electrical signals.

Oscilloscope A machine to show the height and frequency of a sound wave.
Otoscope A medical device used to look inside the ear. More usually called an auriscope.

Percussionist A musician who plays instruments, such as drums or cymbals, by hitting or banging them.
Pitch Sound can be high or low pitch. High pitch sound waves travel more frequently than low pitch sound waves.

Reflect When a sound bounces off a surface.
Seismograph A machine that records sound waves made by movements in thr Earth's crust.
Soft Sounds with low amplitude. Soft sounds have short sound waves.
Solid A solid has a definite shape.
Sound source The object or action that is making a sound.

Sound effects Sounds created artificially to mimic real sounds. Used in plays and films.
Sound barrier Resistance in the air that makes it difficult for aircraft to travel faster than sound.
Sound-proof Something that is sound-proof stops sound travelling through it (for example a wall).
Speed of sound At an air temperature of 20°C sound travels through air at 343 metres per second.
Stethoscope A medical device used to listen to your heartbeat.
Supersonic Faster than the speed of sound.

Tuning fork Two pronged piece of metal that makes a particular musical note when struck.

Ultrasound Very high pitched sound waves that we can't hear. Doctors use ultrasound to look at the inside of the human body and to take pictures of it. Ultrasound can be used to look at a baby in a womb.

Vibration A fast backwards and forwards movement.

Womb The place in a woman's body where a baby grows and develops until it is born.

Index